In its sublimest effect, meditation is an acknowledged pathway to union with universal consciousness. Depending on the tradition through which it is received, meditation takes various forms leading to differences in style and practice. Though the paths are many, the goal is one. The path described here is the mantra meditation of the Raja Yoga tradition, authorised by Guru Deva, Shankaracharya of Jyotirmath, for use by lay people in ordinary life and also known as transcendental meditation. Since its emergence from the East, this discipline has been observed by members of most nationalities, religions and cultures.

In memory of
S. M. Jaiswal
1923 – 2013

MEDITATION

Tinky Brass

@ Tinky Brass 2013
Reprinted 2014
Reprinted 2015
Reprinted 2016
Reprinted 2017
Reprinted 2018 (twice)
Reprinted 2019
Revised and reprinted in 120mm x 180mm format 2021

Copyright @ Tinky Brass 2021

ISBN 978-0-9566309-3-3

Published in Great Britain
By
Kharkadeh
www.kharkadeh.com

CONTENTS

INTRODUCTION

"Meditation is a journey back home; home to the Self"

Here is the experience of a little boy, relocated from central Europe to post-war London where, at five years old, he was enrolled for schooling at St. Mary's Convent, Hampstead. The boy received instruction in prayer and the Catholic vision of heaven and eternity and although he was very young and intellectually unripe, he nevertheless noticed that the nuns drilling the little children did so without conviction; that they had neither insight nor belief in the dogma they dispensed. Disturbed that grown-ups should teach children something they did not understand themselves, the little five-year-old resolved to master the ideas being imparted in order to determine whether they were true or not. In particular, he resolved to understand the concept of eternity – life without end, amen – or as he was taught to say it: 'for ever and ever'.

It was a short walk to the little boy's home – a shared Victorian house on the evens side of Fitzjohn's Avenue – and as soon as he could, he found a quiet corner to sit cross-legged, rest his head in his hands and his elbows on his knees and with all his might, devour, digest and render the meaning of 'for ever'. With eyes shut and faculties entirely focused, he engaged 'for ever' and ever... and ever... andever... andever... resonating within a single determination to know.

In the darkness of his interior, the words turned to sound and then to rhythm, and as the meaning of the words dissolved away, their pulse possessed the little boy, who found himself in a condition of peaceful achievement; a condition he neither understood nor feared and to which he could return whenever he remembered and desired. Through providence, the child had wandered into a conscious experience so pregnant, still and powerfully silent, it left him steeped in the constant awareness that 'this' is not all. It was not until much later, once life had made the child into a man, that returning to the same experience but by a different route, he knew he had been meditating.

And so, the child's insight was companion to the man who found his way back through the practice of mantra meditation. But the man's meditation took consciousness further: the limitless within, resonating with presence and stillness from his childhood, now became golden – golden with the colour of a word written on a leaf...

There was once a saint called Tulsidas who wrote the Hindi Ramayana. He used to live in Benares and while he was sitting on the banks of the Ganges a small boy came crying to the river bank in the evening. He had come to the city to get medicine for his sick mother who was in the town across the river called Rag Nagar. At that time there were no boats available as all the boatmen had gone home. The boy was crying because he was unable to cross to the other bank and didn't know what to do about his ailing mother and her medicine. The saint heard the boy crying and came down to ask what troubled him. The boy told his story. The saint then gave the little boy a leaf, on which was written a Mantra. He told him to hold it in his palm and swim the river; he would have no difficulty in getting across. The boy was very curious and thought he would like to see what had been given to him. He opened his leaf and saw the word written on it. He thought, well, I know this myself and there is no difference between the word I have been given and my own, so I can do it myself. When he tried to swim he found himself swept away by the force of the water. When the saint saw what was happening he called out, "But my dear boy, your word is not going to help you. You asked for help from my word. So take the leaf and hold on to it." The boy in trouble took his advice and crossed the river in safety. [1]

The early steps of spiritual enquiry reveal a gateway onto the universal path that leads back home. Those who take this particular gateway find a living tradition that outreaches history's reckoning and, conducted across time by rare and holy beings like Adi Shankara and Guru Deva, bestows the gift of a mantra, which, like the key to your own heart endowed with the grace of those who carried it before, confers the full transforming power of creation. All this is yours.

Where did the meditation come from? The Creator begins the act of creation with meditation. The meditation comes from the beginning of creation and will only end with creation. [1]

The fundamental causal experience common to all true religions and the source of faith itself, is the simple truth discovered in the innermost peace and quiet stillness of the human heart where the individual is subsumed in the Divine. Here, the one eternal consciousness dwells unseparated, the realisation of which encompasses all knowledge. The journey back home to the Self is the journey into that stillness where the private conscious experience we call life realises the universal conscious experience called God.

SOURCE

The mantra and the method of meditation come from the Indian tradition known as Raja Yoga. 'Yoga' is from the Sanskrit, meaning to join or unite – in English, yoke – referring to the practice of Yoga as the joining or union of Individual Consciousness and Universal Consciousness. 'Raja' is Sanskrit for king; Raja Yoga translates as the king of Yogas.

The purpose of mantra meditation is to take individual awareness into a condition of stillness in which experience of higher consciousness becomes possible. In preparation for this, the traditional path in former times required the aspirant to complete successive steps of self-control and discipline as grounding for receiving the method of meditation. Those steps, formulated by the sage Patanjali in the Yoga Sutras, are progressive physical and psychological disciplines, leading eventually to initiation into meditation. These disciplines are for those who can follow them rigorously in a cloistered and dedicated life. For busy people in modern times, and for those who integrate the spiritual path into their worldly duties in what is known as The Fourth Way, practising the meditation in itself introduces and crystallises the effects of the preparatory steps previously required. The Eightfold System of Yoga described below, illustrates the depth of undertaking expected of those who went before and laid the foundations of the tradition of meditation which is now available to all. The steps are:

1 Yama   Rules for the physical body and actions in daily life, including veracity, pacifism, contentment, celibacy and poverty.

2 Niyama   Rules for the subtle body in daily life including knowledge of the scriptures, purity of thought, measured thoughts and surrender through understanding.

3 Asana   Discipline to maintain health of the body through posture.

4 Pranayama Mastery of bodily energies including the breath, to aid health of body and mind.

5 Pratyahara Detatchment from external and internal influences.

6 Dharana   Single pointed attention. To be able to hold the attention on an idea or object without deflecting.

7 Dhyana   To meditate and, with the mantra's guidance, dive into the deep realms of the being so that the mantra, meditation and meditator all become one. Here one learns to cut off even the subtle body's activities and enter the Causal level.

8 Samadhi   Oneness. Where there is Consciousness only. Here, individual consciousness is so unencumbered, free and light, it naturally merges with Universal Consciousness.

Not until the aspirant demonstrated success in all the stages up to the sixth, Dharana, and was able to hold attention on an idea or object continuously, was he considered ready for stages seven and eight and worthy of initiation into mantra meditation. This is a hard and full-time discipline and many serious people have given their lives to it, considering the price paid as nothing compared with the treasure realised. This system has endured in the East for over twenty centuries, providing seekers of truth with the means to realise the source of all. Today's legacy, the boon of all their efforts, is the endurance of the tradition.

> *God is always present, and in the same way the meditation is always present and has been present since the beginning of history. The Absolute is Eternal, the Knowledge is Eternal.... Meditation has existed all through the creation, but given differently in different ages. Just now, Realised Men have made it available to many more people because of the needs of the time; that is how you heard of it.* [1]

After the unprecedented horrors of global war that marked the first half of the twentieth century, it was decided to make the benefits of eastern wisdom generally available to the West in the form of a simple discipline that ordinary householders could integrate into a busy day. A renowned saint, The Shankaracharya of Jyotirmath, His Holiness Swami Brahmananda Saraswati, affectionately known as Guru Deva, was instrumental in approving the mantra from Raja Yoga for this purpose. It was resolved to offer the discipline of mantra meditation and the holy rite of initiation to all and any who desired it and, acknowledging that westerners would be wholly unprepared in the traditional path, the mantra chosen was one whose influence would compensate for the absent foundations of a highly disciplined life. As well as its primary object of guiding the individual awareness towards Self-Realisation, the influence of the mantra had to be capable of ameliorating those negative tendencies which formerly would have been a bar to initiation.

> *Previously they were made to practise these steps one after another and then they were considered fit to enter the realm of the seventh step. But now we start with the seventh step... ....all the Seven Steps are brought together in a gentler way suitable to householder, different from yogis or ascetics who are specialists or full-time practitioners.* [1]

Consequently, the holiest name in the Hindu canon was made available for the benefit of all. In 1960, a contact was established with Guru Deva's principal disciple and appointed successor as Shankaracharya of Jyotirmath, His Holiness Swami Shantananda Saraswati. Over the following thirty-seven years, Swami Shantananda Saraswati expounded the principles of the universal philosophy underlying the meditation – Advaita – to representatives from three international schools of spiritual philosophy based in London.*

---

* The School of Economic Science, The Study Society and The School of Meditation.

THE COMMON EXPERIENCE

Normal life does not permit access to the deep and quiet stillness in which higher levels of conscious experience are known. Just as the intensity of sunlight obliterates the ever-present stars, so the intensity of the active mind overwhelms this inner peace. That deep peace, described in The Bible as '*the peace which passeth all understanding*' (Philippians 4:7) exists below the range of everyday mind. The Self can only experience it if awareness is liberated from the tyranny of thoughts. Thoughts can only think; they cannot experience their own absence. It is not possible to quell thoughts by thinking.

> *When one knows that one is still, one is not still; and when one knows one is at peace, one is still away from it because the great barrier is still there – to recognise 'I' and its relation with peace and stillness. In complete peace or stillness there is no 'I'.* [1]

Mantra meditation guides the individual on a journey inwards to the Self. Each meditation reprises that journey, either picking up from before or starting afresh. Progress requires single-minded attention, like the little five-year-old in the introduction. A story is told to illustrate this. The story tells of a king who, having decided to retire to the jungle, pledges his kingdom to whoever will meet him at the appointed time. The story is an allegory of meditation – the individual Self travelling inwards to realise union with the universal Self, and the obstacles to be avoided on the way:

A king who had grown old decided to abdicate his throne and to go to the jungle for practising penance. He announced that he would give his Kingdom to any person who would come to him by 4 o'clock. Everybody heard the announcement and thought it a good idea to go and meet him at 4 o'clock.

In his capital city the King put beautiful shops containing everything that can be had, jewellery, gold, silks, toys, everything that anybody could want to have. And at every gate and in every quarter, there were people to give away all these things, without payment, all free! And finally there was a big sleeping room containing voluptuous appointments and bedding.

Thousands of people started out to go and get the Kingdom which the King had promised to give away, but they were persuaded to go to the shops and take whatever they wanted free, and enjoy themselves. At all these places, people stopped to help themselves, and lost time or forgot their quest. But one man overcame all these temptations; without letting anyone dissuade him he just went through and met the King at the appointed time and demanded the Kingdom, which the King duly gave him. [1]

It should be possible to keep the attention on such a magnificent prize and avoid the obvious traps, but it seems that the lure of distractions is gravely underestimated. The compulsion to engage with temptations encountered on the way to meet the king in this story represents a particular function of individual psychology – the inability to switch off the internal monologue. This is the compulsion to engage with the habitual review of themes and memories that are examined so regularly and are so intimately familiar, that they never age, grow up, wear out, change or depart. This autonomous musing, to which the individual has become so attached, forms a mental cage which is only noticed when one tries to leave it.

Continuous conscious thought is so embedded in the human experience, so ingrained in waking activity, that it has an absolute stranglehold that is almost unassailable. The persistence of mind automatically causes thinking to re-establish itself immediately and continuously; it cannot rest intentionally. Focusing the attention in mantra meditation, however, is a technique that enables consciousness to experience itself unencumbered and free, but the task of mantra meditation, leading the meditator from continuous mental activity to complete conscious stillness, means transcending the archetypal characteristic that defines humanity. This is a huge undertaking so, especially in the early stages, the common experience is that meditation is practised with sincerity but without reaching the sublime levels that transcend thought. Nevertheless, even at this level, meditating on a transformative mantra is beneficial:

> *...it is quite possible that one may not enter the silence, and even if one did, one may be out very soon. This stage is creating a level, so every minute of it is of value, although one may not be able to recognise what is happening inside.* [1]

The sound qualities of the mantra carry a subtle

influence, the effects of which are evident from the outset. These qualities cleanse impurities, enhance and encourage goodness and provide a lightness of peace and knowledge. When repeated inwardly, these influences permeate every part of the individual.

> *The sound of the Mantra has been given to us through the Vedic tradition and its roots are in the Brahman itself. All these pure sounds which are incorporated in the Mantra are full of qualities, each sound has a particular element or meaning, which combine to create a particular type of effect, when this Mantra is being repeated by the individual. Thus, the meaning of the Mantra and its proper pronunciation by the meditator internally will have the proper effect which is embodied in the sound of the Mantra itself. First of all it eliminates all the impure, unnecessary and harmful traits in the individual, or in his inner being, secondly it increases and develops whatever good he holds within himself. Thirdly, it makes the individual much more universal. There is a process of expansion which takes place in his inner being so that he becomes much more universal and becomes more united and in tune with the universe. These are the factors which crystallise through the Mantra. As far as the individual is concerned, certainly purity of heart is a good pre-condition for the Mantra to work much more than it would with an impure heart.*
>
> *The third factor concerns the tradition. The tradition makes a Mantra much more potent*

because it has been evolved through the centuries and millennia and been practised by great saints, the forces of these saints have been passed from one to the other, from teacher to disciple. There is this type of force which comes through the tradition. [1]

20

MIND

The deepest meditation comes in Dhyana and Samadhi. These steps do not exist in the mind. Meditation leads consciousness into an interior world that has no limits, edges or borders – as big as the universe itself – and is entirely unknown. This interior world keeps its own laws which are beyond comprehension and are impervious to examination by the ordinary mind. This interior world cannot be described or known in the conventional sense. It is experienced by the Self alone.

The human mind is the gate that blocks the entrance to this inner world, and the human mind does not like meditating. The active mind counters efforts to meditate in a simple and effective way – it induces sleep, either the physical sleep in which one dreams, or metaphorical sleep, in which one daydreams. Just as one remembers waking up but is never aware of falling asleep, so one always remembers re-starting the journey inward but is never conscious of stopping on the way. An example of metaphorical sleep is described in this extract:

> ...reading a book or newspaper and discovering that although you have read to the bottom of the page, you recall nothing because you have been daydreaming; something has triggered an association and one element of the mind fantasised about the idea while the other element of the mind mechanically followed the printed page. [4]

As the activity of reading progresses, the attention

departs from the meaning of the words. The focus of attention gets caught by a dream, and the reader daydreams while simultaneously following the words on the page, remembering nothing of what was read. Such simple forgetting happens because the normal apparatus for experiencing consciousness directs the focus of awareness through several functions that can work independently of each other.

The eastern system, with its centuries' deep immersion in spiritual philosophy and normal psychology coupled with profound insight, has arrived at an analysis of the psyche that is helpful, practical and easily recognisable. Some familiarity with it answers fundamental questions about meditation.

This system identifies four discrete functions that collectively constitute human consciousness. To avoid misunderstanding arising from translation, these functions are called by their Sanskrit names: Manas, Buddhi, Chitta and Ahankara. Each of these functions is described as having a true and legitimate purpose which is universal, benevolent and altruistic; an ideal that is rarely known. And also a distorted use – how they are normally experienced – the result of the function being pressed into service of individual, small-minded, personal and selfish considerations.

> *There are four streams which constitute the inner world...these four functions which are known as Manas, Buddhi, Chitta and Ahankara.*
>
> *Manas is the mouthpiece of desires; through this all desires are expressed before senses take over to act.*
>
> *Buddhi is that which discriminates... it gives*

directions as to what is useful and harmful to the Self.

Chitta is that which holds all the knowledge of the Individual (Memory) and cherishes certain thoughts. It is the store where continuity is maintained in order to fulfil desire. It always keeps reminded of the line of action.

Ahankara (Individual Ego) is the Individual Self which gives the feeling of existence. The feeling of "I" "I am doing", etc.

All these four are subject to corruption and weakness. [1]

Knowledge of these elements of the psyche, what they do and how they interact, has helped countless people with questions about the technique of meditation as well as questions encountered in everyday life. A brief description of each follows:

Manas

Manas is the mechanical mind whose function is to carry information from the senses to the intellect and to convey instructions from the intellect to the organs of action. Manas has no capacity for discrimination or judgement; it is simply the messenger between the inner and the outer. The defining characteristic by which Manas is readily identified is its assertive, intense strength. Think of it as a servant with limitless energy, thickset and powerful but lacking any ability to discriminate or assess. It works without stopping or pausing, promoting the function of the senses in an unchecked stream of desire. Manas is the instrument that propels habits; it guides the organs of action, regardless of whether or not they act in accord with one's better judgement. For example, when the senses note something pleasant, Manas says 'desirable, want it'. When the senses note something horrifying, Manas stares. Manas issues the prompts to repeat habitual activity. Any physical, emotional or intellectual activity about which one could say: 'I know I shouldn't, but...' or 'I wish I could stop...' illustrates the role of Manas in controlling unfavourable behaviour. Recognising Manas explains why the 'I' who speaks such words of regret and the 'I' who acts contrary to them, appear to be completely different entities. In the archetypal image of the conflicted person with a good angel on one shoulder and a bad angel on the other, the bad angel represents the role of Manas.

The organs of sense work more or less automatically, supplying knowledge and information of the world. When indulgence in that knowledge is confused with receipt of the knowledge, one becomes the unwitting creature of desire. Those who indulge the impulses they receive from the senses contrary to their better judgement or heartfelt desire, live under the dominion of an out-of-control servant who has taken over the household. Awaking to the need to change this relationship, one often resolves to tackle the challenge at significant milestones – New Year's resolutions for example – and it is at these times that the persistence of Manas as an obstacle is encountered.

That is the common experience of Manas. There is another way to experience Manas; an ideal state which arises when Manas is pure. In its purified state, Manas is the

good and faithful servant who knows his master and brings
to attention only what is right. He observes the impositions
of his role and respects the authority of his master – you
– serving only your best interests. People who display the
characteristics associated with a disciplined Manas are often
described as having strength of character. Purified and
stilled, the ideal experience of Manas is described like this:

> *A condition of sameness would possess your heart.*
> *The mind would shed its burden and become*
> *filled with joy instead. A feeling of perfection and*
> *limitlessness would supervene.* [1]

Buddhi

Buddhi is described as intellect, higher mind or
discrimination. Its function is to know what is right. When
the individual needs to know which choice to select, how
to act in any sphere, whether it is choosing the colour of
shoes or deciding how to vote, it is Buddhi that informs
the decision. In the previous example of Manas conveying
the message from the senses, Buddhi's function is to review
the message and decide right or wrong, yes or no, good or
bad etc.

Although Buddhi naturally cleaves to goodness and
rightness, it is delicate and easily bruised. Any sort of abuse
or mistreatment will leave it addled and confused. Abuse
of Buddhi comes in the form of lies and insincerity. For
example, if one lies to oneself about something, or makes up
spurious explanations and excuses to justify something one
knows to be wrong, Buddhi becomes confused.

As the needle in a compass always points to the

North, so Buddhi always points to the Truth. If, however, Buddhi is required to acknowledge a substitute or fake truth, it gets disoriented and points elsewhere. Just as a compass is confused by iron, Buddhi is confused by lies and insincerity. In time, Buddhi ceases to recognise truth and becomes agitated looking here and there, like someone who is lost.

Buddhi's relation to truth is innate so, although it is sometimes described as intellect, intellectualising is no help to it. Recognition of truth by Buddhi is direct and immediate; overthinking can get in the way and be confusing. Similarly, conclusions based on emotional preferences undermine Buddhi, leaving it weak and resulting in, for example, otherwise intelligent and well-educated people disagreeing on basic issues of right and wrong, good and bad. One can appeal to another person's Buddhi through reason, but when Buddhi is influenced by emotional imperatives, it is unreceptive to reason. It is futile to attempt to correct that in anyone other than oneself.

To some extent we all bargain with truth and maintain a perilous balance between what we acknowledge is right and what we would prefer to be right, believing that just a little compromise causes only a little harm. For those on any sort of spiritual search or path in pursuit of True Knowledge, purifying Buddhi is an essential first step because without a purified Buddhi it is impossible to spot the difference between True Knowledge and its countless imposters.

As a manifestation of Higher Knowledge, faith is a form of awareness that emerges when Buddhi is clear enough to acknowledge essential goodness. Those who lack faith, distrust Higher Knowledge, preferring the familiarity of more concrete yardsticks for determining morality. The relation of faith to pure Buddhi is primary, as in this answer to a question on how to purify Buddhi:

> *Love the Truth, and leave the untruth. That is the cure.* [1]

By cultivating a relationship with truth, not through knowing, or understanding, or logic, or cleverness, but through love, Buddhi is sheltered in the domain of truth, from where it will not mislead. Then, faith – not the blind faith of the fanatic, but faith as perception born of clear vision – enables one to recognise the value of simple advice like "*Love the truth; leave the untruth*" the understanding of which deepens with practice.

When Buddhi is secure and confident in its love for truth, it stops searching about and becomes still. Moments of indecision no longer arise; Buddhi knows what is right and what is wrong and acts without reservation. People who display characteristics associated with a still Buddhi are sometimes described as moral.

Pure Buddhi is like a headlight on a dark road: it illuminates the way ahead; it manifests wisdom and turns faith into love. When Buddhi is pure, it opens the gate for the individual to see their own real Self – the realm of Truth, Consciousness and Bliss.

> *Knowledge of Truth strengthens man's belief in the Truth, throws light on the individual and on life.*

Things become clear; every leaf on a tree becomes a
page of a holy book to one whose eyes are open to the
knowledge of God... This man has not seen God, but
he has seen the reflection of God in man, and when
this is so, then everything that comes from this man
comes from God himself. [5]

Chitta

Chitta is the place where experience is collected and
stored. All recalled, latent and archetypal memories are kept
here. The characteristics which constitute the nature of an
individual, and by which an individual is recognised and
known, are all kept in Chitta.

Chitta could be called a memory bank or a depository.
It has been described as a grand library set in a classical edifice
housing all knowledge. The interior of this depository is
unlit and soundless, with thoughts, memories and attitudes
arranged on shelves in ranks and aisles stretching deep into
the distant darkness. The impressive front doors have long
since seized up and no longer work, so access is through a
small side door. Cobwebs and dry darkness occupy the aisles,
forgotten books lie torn and open on the floor, furniture
and files clutter the intersections. Only paths, picked out in
the dust, indicate where those facts, attitudes and memories
that are loved and cherished by the individual are habitually
visited. All speech originates from the nature stored in
Chitta. The result of all speech and action returns here.

There is another door to this dark and dusty
interior; an unseen back door that is never completely
shut, leaving a gap through which grace enters. This door

is not acknowledged in ordinary life but once found, can be opened from within or without. When it begins to open freely, one sees that it is not just a door: the entire back wall opens with it, and the side walls open too and also the ceiling and the floor, and light streams in, illuminating all and everything. When Chitta is pure, everything happens without attachment; events leave no mark. Pure Chitta is clear and transparent and shines with the light of the Self.

Ahankara

Ahankara is the feeling of existence, the sense of 'I'. The closest English word would be ego.

As with the other elements of the psyche, Ahankara is experienced in a limited form that facilitates individualism. Each morning the Self wakes into the experience of 'I' am. This 'I' is an expression of universal consciousness on the individual scale, i.e. each individual is their own universe and experiences consciousness from that premise. The experience of 'I' has all the acknowledged qualities of separateness, uniqueness, autonomy etc., that are expected of oneself and of others as the norm. The inner world of other people is considered to be as inviolable and impenetrable as one's own, so Ahankara is experienced as an effective barrier to communion of being, and gives rise to a private facade that assumes different roles depending on which particular desire, characteristic or situation has prominence.

This feeling of separate identity is unchallenged except for those rare moments of grace when a veil is drawn aside and individual awareness is suffused with universality. People who experience this as flashes of insight, describe it in many different, sometimes contradictory, ways due to the lack of a common 'language of the soul'. Nevertheless, Ahankara is a sense of being that identifies as consciousness (Chitta) discriminating mind (Buddhi) and mechanical mind (Manas) in turn, but which, in the light of true knowledge, is known to be none of these. When pure, Ahankara sees the true essence of everything as the reflection of one universal consciousness. Within and without it is the same consciousness reflected everywhere:

> *If you begin to be what you are, you will realise everything. But to begin to be what you are, you must come out of what you are not. You are not those thoughts which are turning, turning in your mind; you are not those changing feelings; you are not the different decisions you make and the different wills you have; you are not that separate ego. Well then, what are you?*
>
> *You will find, when you have come out of what you are not, that the ripple on the water is whispering to you: "I am That"; the birds in the trees are singing to you: "I am That"; the moon and the stars are shining beacons to you: "I am That". For you are in everything in the world, and everything in the world is in you, and at the same time you are that – everything.* [1]

Manas & Buddhi

Ideally, Manas and Buddhi would work in concert with Manas bringing information for consideration by Buddhi; Buddhi deciding how to respond and Manas executing that decision obediently. In practice, the message Manas brings is consistently to attend to habitual and mechanical imperatives, for example, physical habits like smoking or snacking, intellectual habits like replays of past remorse or celebration, and ego-bolstering habits like affirmation of entitlement and righteousness. Manas delivers this inexorable stream of reminders which pop up in the awareness, and Buddhi then discriminates.

> *We all discriminate – we assess what we encounter in life and make selections accordingly. Usually we discriminate for ourselves on the basis of what brings satisfaction, so we choose the food we enjoy, view images that please us, listen to music that moves us, associate with people who validate us, wear clothes that suit us and so on; it's fairly easy to know what satisfies. Now, if for example the doctor says to take exercise because it is beneficial or avoid cigarettes because they are harmful, then you are required to choose not what satisfies but what brings benefit, and you experience a conflict arising between two elements – one being what you want and the other being what is right.* [4]

And so a tussle ensues between a fragile Buddhi promoting what is right and a powerful Manas promoting gratification. Only if one is honest, can one identify those areas where Manas prevails and Buddhi is browbeaten into promoting a lower standard of personal values than it would prefer. If Buddhi cannot make its voice heard and remains weak and unassertive, Manas will take over the

role of Buddhi and Buddhi will cease to be able to tell right
from wrong.

> *A weak Buddhi loses control over Manas and the*
> *man becomes a slave to momentary desires of*
> *pleasure. If one is prone to such desires, the Buddhi*
> *will protest according to its strength. If it failed and*
> *Manas had his way to momentary pleasure and,*
> *having seen the bad result of the desired action,*
> *Buddhi would once again remind of the harm done*
> *to Self. A weak man forgets all this again and does*
> *the same harmful but momentarily pleasant act*
> *again and again. Such men are doomed. If one's*
> *Buddhi is pure and strong, it will keep check on the*
> *Manas and allow only those desires to be acted upon*
> *which are useful to the Self.* [1]

The value of this model of the psyche is in its ready
application to everyday experience. Through recognition
of the two interactive elements in oneself – the dynamic,
assertive Manas and the passive, reflective Buddhi – they
become familiar. This distinction clarifies the practicalities
of entry into meditation.

In the example of reading a book or newspaper and
simultaneously daydreaming, it is Manas that mechanically
follows the page while the Buddhi daydreams. In meditation,
both Buddhi and Manas should come to rest. Buddhi comes
to rest when it is not agitated by Manas. Manas however, will
not rest; it is called quicksilver or mercury by the alchemists
because it is always moving.

The whole process of making gold is described by the alchemists in a symbolical way. They say gold is made out of mercury; the nature of mercury is to be ever moving, but by a certain process the mercury is first stilled, and once stilled it becomes silver; the silver then has to be melted, and on to the melted silver, the juice of a herb is poured, and then the melted silver turns into gold …. The real interpretation of this process is that mercury represents the nature of the ever-restless mind realised especially when a man tries to collect his attention …. Such is the nature of mind, it becomes more restless when you desire to control it; like mercury it is constantly moving. [5]

The technique of mantra meditation is precisely for this: to bring Manas and Buddhi to stillness.

PREPARATION

*One enters into meditation, and the only thing
one has to do is to reach that state of total stillness
where the mantra, meditation and meditator merge
into one undifferentiated unity.*[1]

The trajectory of an arrow is determined at the point
of aim. Once it has left the bow, it flies with the intention and
determination invested at the outset. So it is in meditation.
The aim and purpose in meditation should be free and clear.
The instruction for meditators is simple: Sit with a straight
back, close the eyes and lips, repeat the mantra inwardly and
follow where it takes you. One should be prepared do this
with the attitude that, for the duration of this meditation,
all memories, cares, worries, hopes, fears, expectations etc.,
have fallen to the ground and one has stepped out of them.
They can be dealt with later on.

The time of day set aside for meditation and the
location can make a difference; certain times are particularly
receptive and some places are peaceful, so attending to these
will help, but time and place are not necessarily one's to
choose. So long as meditating frames the day and the place
is undisturbed, aim and intention will make up for the rest.
One element of preparation however, is always in one's gift:

*...one should prepare the body before meditation.
There are three places of importance – the hands,
mouth and the eyes. Through hand passes the energy,
in mouth we repeat the Mantra, and the eyes take in
the light. We must clean these properly before sitting
for meditation.*[1]

Cleaning the hands, mouth and eyes makes a difference symbolically. Energy flowing in through the hands is not impeded if the hands aren't clean but having clean hands acknowledges intention and respect.

Blindness is the universal metaphor for ignorance – being in the dark, unable to see. The light spoken of in the extract above is exactly the same light spoken of in St. John's Gospel: '*And the light shineth in darkness; and the darkness comprehended it not*,' i.e. truth is cloaked by ignorance. This condition, of reality obscured by illusion, governs the world we know. When the illusion is removed, the truth shines through...

> *When I was at Catalina Island off Los Angeles I was with a group of 80 people that Maharishi was training as meditation guides. We meditated for 7 hours twice a day... ...one morning I experienced a lift in consciousness that revealed to me what lay behind the surface of everything.*
>
> *I am telling you this because it made me look at [the spiritual organisation] which I was in then, quite differently. I saw that each individual had to become aware of themselves to discover what was true and what was false... that everything we have thought about ourselves is an illusion.*
>
> *Meditation takes place when there is no thought of ourselves as this physical embodiment. Only when we become aware of the truth that we ourselves live in everything and encompass everything can we begin to understand what meditation is. I was*

shown over and over again that the meaning and purpose of life is love. In the heart is a place where this love is reflected. Love is universal, belongs to no one, yet is given from above freely. [2]

The mouth is where the mantra begins its silent journey, so cleaning the mouth, keeping it free of lies and deception is fundamental to receiving the mantra with sincerity, as one would receive a friend, a lover, a saint or one's own conscience.

Conscience is the light of the Soul that is burning within the chambers of your heart.

It is the little spark of celestial fire which makes known to you the presence of the Indweller, the author of the Divine laws of Truth and Holiness.

It raises the voice of protest whenever anything is thought or done contrary to the interest of its Master.

Conscience is the voice of the Self which says 'yes' or 'no' when you are involved in a moral struggle.

It is a call from within to do an act, or avoid it.

Conscience is the internal monitor.

Conscience is a form of truth.

Conscience is like a silent teacher.

It is the inner voice without sound.

It is very delicate and easily stifled.

It is so very clear that it is impossible to mistake it.

Cowardice asks, 'Is it safe?'

Avarice asks, 'Is there any gain in it?'

Vanity asks, 'Can I become famous?'

Lust asks, 'Is there pleasure?'
But Conscience asks, 'Is it right?'
A glad clear conscience is the temple of God. [3]

These preparations should not be made a great issue; they are only to facilitate meditation. They help initially but, once you have reached the inner quiet, these preparations will have no effect on you. Then you can meditate anywhere and at any time; meditation itself takes care of everything else.

THE FIRST STAGE

There is a story that tells how the ever-active Manas is stilled. In the story, the role of Manas is represented by a ghost which has been captured by a man in order to work for him as a servant...

...he gained control of the ghost in order to use it like a servant. But this ghost was very powerful, and very quick. When asked to do something, the ghost was very quick to complete the tasks, and then returned for more orders. Before the ghost had taken on the job it had said that if there was no work, it would devour the man. This was the condition – it must be kept busy all the time. This man thought there was plenty to do, so the ghost could be kept busy like a human being, but the ghost was so fast that very soon it finished all the work the man could think of.

Now this man had an inspiration and he said to himself that with the quickness of this ghost it is impossible to give it enough jobs so it should be given some job which it must attend to all the time, but which would never come to an end. He got an idea and asked the ghost to cut a bamboo pole and bring it to him. He asked the ghost to fix the bamboo pole in the courtyard. When the ghost had fixed it firmly there, the man said 'Unless I ask you to come and do a special job, your general job is to go up and down on this pole.' Now going continually up and down this pole exhausted the ghost very quickly, and then it settled down at the bottom of the pole to wait for the next order

Now Manas is very like a ghost – its job is to propose and counter-propose – there is no end to the variety of propositions it can produce. This is the job of the Manas, and that is how it keeps people busy, and people get tired, not only mentally, but physically.

The pole is the Mantra. Order the Manas there and it will settle down fairly quickly. [1]

Repeating the mantra to quieten thoughts and travel inwards is like negotiating one's way past an overbearing secretary to get access to the boss. Once contact with the boss is established, the way through is clear and one need no longer worry about the secretary. The mantra settles Manas by giving it alternative work to do. By engaging Manas in repeating the mantra, one avoids the trap of 'thinking' the mantra. Thinking is the province of Buddhi and Buddhi should be inactive in meditation.

In the realm of meditation there is no activity of Buddhi, we surrender the activity of Buddhi. It is only in the outward world that we have to use the activity of Buddhi. [1]

Setting Manas to repeat the mantra relieves Buddhi and permits it to be still. Buddhi must be completely inactive for meditation to be effective.

There is a natural way of reciting the mantra. We realise the recitation is going on in Manas. The lips

*are not moving but the recitation is going on in
Manas as we feel it. All the time our hearts should
be able to listen. Hrdaya – heart – should be able to
listen to the sound of the mantra although the mouth
does not produce any sound. As long as we feel that
the recitation is going on then we are deriving some
benefit from it.* [1]

Setting Manas to repeat the mantra and letting
Buddhi fall still is the first stage of meditation. The mantra
replaces the psychological activity that monopolises
awareness, allowing it to pass the barrier that blocks the
entrance to the inner world where meditation happens.

There is no need to guide or desire one's awareness to
enter the limitless world within because awareness naturally
belongs there. Once the way is free, it will return there
automatically just as the pressurised air in a party balloon
returns to the atmosphere – its natural home – once it is
released.

With the relaxation of the body and the settling
of Manas and Buddhi, awareness dives inwards and the
mantra slows and quietens. In its coarsest form, the mantra
manifests as audible

Sound. This is the level at which the mantra is given
and received at initiation. The mantra's subtle form, which
is used in meditation, is unmanifest sound, so no audible
sound is made but its essential quality resonates in the
subtle world; the world of the mind. The subtle form of the
mantra endures while the practice is established and, once
the awareness has bypassed the mind, the root of the mantra
– its causal quality – remains as an emotional pulse which

gradually diminishes the deeper it goes.

    The guiding hand that brings the meditator to the door of the inner world, itself becomes the finer hand from within to take the meditation deeper. The mantra manifests at the levels through which awareness passes, so as it leads inwards it becomes finer. Holding on to the coarser form of the mantra (sounding the mantra internally) prevents this natural refinement. Like the love letter that brought a lover to the presence of his beloved, one should enjoy the introduction, and let go of the means of achieving it.

> *A certain man, when his beloved let him sit beside her, produced a letter and read it to her. In the letter were verses and praise and lamentation and many humble entreaties. The beloved said: "If this is for my sake, to read this at the time of meeting is to waste one's life. I am here beside you, and you are reading a letter! This is not the mark of true lovers."* [6]

Meditation takes individual consciousness into the presence of the True Self. The True Self encompasses all, so experience here requires merging all in all; the meditator, the mantra, the meditation – all become one.

> *Howsoever subtle the sound may be it exists because of the movement, and as long as there is movement there is separation. Thus the climax of meditation is that one becomes One. There is nothing else. Only one without a second.* [1]

When meditation is sustained and deep, profound

stillness settles on the body. There may be physical sensations, the result of energy (Pranas) settling and the centre of consciousness rising. These sensations occur when the physical body becomes more relaxed than usual, leaving the energy pathways open. The advice is always to ignore them. One sensation, which becomes familiar and which settles on the being in deep meditation, is the presence of profound inner peace; an experience which stays with the meditator. In time, this feeling alone is sufficient to usher the awareness into the silence. It has no description but it is natural, it is recognised and remembered.

> So it is suggested that when you are about to meditate you collect your body and put it into a comfortable position so that it will keep you going for the required time of meditation without hindrance. We close the eyes to put out the external world; we put out all sounds coming to us, so that we sever all relationship with the external world and then we come to the moving thoughts which keep on visiting us, and we keep on trying to dis-associate from these dear thoughts (which visit us very closely) with the help of the Mantra. [1]

The boon of passing the first stage of meditation comes when the mantra moves to the heart. This is not the physical heart but that place in the centre of the chest between the sternum and the throat where spiritual consciousness first begins to resonate. The relationship with the mantra becomes intimate and loving and the mantra becomes indistinguishable from the Self. Its presence is felt all the time and meditation becomes a joyful meeting approached with natural happiness.

> *Once during meditation one gets the taste of inner happiness which is not available in the physical world, then one wants to have it again and again. In the same way you can drop a few grains of sugar, you do not have to create a road for the ant to travel from one grain to another. Once it has tasted the sugar the ant will find its way to the next grain. It is the same for oneself. Once one gets the taste of inner happiness then one does not need anyone's help because one is capable of taking the journey oneself.* [1]

When asked for proof of the existence of God, a wise man answered that the very existence of the question, not to say the questioner, was proof enough. Nevertheless, if further proof were required it should be understood that this is the sort of knowledge that cannot be passed from one person to another; it can only be realised by the individual for, and from, their own experience. So, for example, if a man lives far inland and asks for proof of the existence of the sea, how can one who knows the sea prove that it exists or what its nature is? The advice for such a man can only be to take a certain road and follow it to the end where he will find and experience the great ocean of bliss for himself. No other advice will provide the experience. Taking that road is not easy but it is simple and well within the ability of anyone who wants to experience the answer to the perennial questions. Having been told where the road leads, the individual must complete the journey to realise the experience directly.

> *Meditation leads men to discharge their pains and realise full bliss. This is the zenith of human endeavour and in it is hidden the secret of human progress.* [1]

TRADITION

It is natural to want improvement, and the benefits of meditation whether social, psychological or physical are well documented. But the true goal of meditation – to take the individual consciousness into the light of universal consciousness – requires that meditation is not separate from the rest of life but is integrated into the life of the meditator and becomes their spiritual path. This is possible in the modern age in a way that was not possible in times past.

> To create any permanent result, there must always be a system, and one must go through the system with proper steps to get the required result... Thus one has to learn to regulate activities and obey certain rules of conduct; learn to sit quietly and properly without making much movement, and regulate the breathing system; leave all worldly thoughts out, and learn to hold one idea in the mind; and only then is the initiate allowed to meditate. This is a hard System and only the brave can take it, even under a worthy guide. The same System is to a great degree shortened in the way we give meditation today; but in doing meditation all the same steps will have to be accomplished in the end. [1]

The demands of the traditional path and the disciplines it imposes are quite alien to western householders and realistically, are improbable goals for any except those living a monastic or hermitic life. Nevertheless, experienced

meditators become familiar with the changes described
in the Eightfold System of Yoga because their effects are
observable.

The subtle changes in the inner and outer life of
meditators regulate behaviour in the same way that the
traditional path in former times required. For example,
experienced meditators report that worldly dictates make
way as the spontaneous prompt to meditate arises, and that
during the early stages of meditation, one's posture and
breath are naturally corrected. The stillness in meditation
affecting the third step, Asana (control of posture) has been
illustrated like this:

> One can see it in the activities and dispositions of
> such men who provide themselves with Spiritual
> rest... the physical movements of such people are
> only geared to the natural rhythm, and the result
> is simplicity and economy of movement. They
> never rush into any situation; are never agitated;
> and perform all actions in an efficient, sublime and
> refined way. Whatever they do will emerge from
> stillness, be held in stillness, and again submerge in
> the same stillness which they experience in this great
> total immobility. [1]

Following on from the early stages, one discovers
a sense of detachment that repels habitual intrusions
and helps to maintain attention – something that is
otherwise impossible. These changes are delicate and may
go unnoticed initially. Transformation of the inner and
outer life of a meditator is not automatic; expectation of
change is essential, so one will not evolve if evolution is

unwelcome. The transformative effect of the mantra is most potent when change is embraced. This becomes evident as one feels a difference in one's external behaviour, how one relates to honesty or selflessness. Similarly, the effect on the subtle world when one notices the mantra coming to mind during the day accompanied by a feeling of companionship, familiarity and optimism. Subtle influences show in the voice and speech of those who meditate effectively and one would notice worldly values gradually lose their hold. Matters seem more simple, less urgent.

> When we wake up from a sleep, the sensory world stands up before us as it is. When we perceive a dream, however, it is a dream-world that we see. When we go into deep and dreamless sleep, then everything of the world merges into the Self, and only that Self is, all in all. That is why we try to merge everything into our own Self in our day-to-day life. The advantage of this would be that the thought of the past and of the future would weaken and you would find yourself in a special state of Selfconsciousness. [1]

LIMITLESS WITHIN

*Meditation is going back home – home to the
Self. What the teacher can do is to describe the
journey from start to finish and show what usually
happens and what may be met on the way... – he
does not have to stop and enquire but go direct to
the Absolute...* [1]

Having bypassed the obstacle of the mind and entered
the deep peace within, external advice and assistance stops.
It is said that the guide who shows the lover to the place
of the beloved stops at the door; only the lover enters. The
guide has fulfilled his duty so he turns back and the union is
only of the lover and the beloved. Similarly, help, advice and
guidance in meditation is for the first part of the journey
only. Beyond that, one is in the care of the Self.

*This is a journey of the individual consciousness
inwards to the Universal Consciousness, the
Absolute. One starts the mantra, and repeats
the mantra, one initiates this at the level of the
personality, and then this repetition of the mantra
is leading on to the bare thread of meditation which
is the Dharana.*

*This movement is aimed at only one thing, and
that is to cut out or diminish the activity involved
in life. Although it is known as the "practice of
meditation", yet this "practice" is leading towards
the end of all activity. Slowly and gradually this
march towards nonactivity takes place until one*

reaches the realm of Union (Yoga) which is stillness or unity of both outer and inner worlds. This is the experience of Self as universal; here there is no duality and there remains no place to move on to, and there is no time to change to, for He is the place, the time and also the substance. In that profound silence, stillness or Yoga, all movements stop, and there is only 'One without a second'. [1]

Preparation for this union or Yoga, is where knowledge of help and advice is applied. For the union to be experienced however, all must be relinquished. Every type of temporal knowledge – information, wisdom, philosophy etc. – has its being within the realm of duality, and it is through wisdom, philosophy etc. that the nature, structure and values of duality are sustained. Knowledge, requiring both a subject and an object, means that two elements persist. The ultimate goal of meditation is realisation of the Absolute as Self, not as knowledge. This realisation is the heart of the experience called Advaita.

In English, Advaita means not-dual – One – nothing else. Paradoxically, the nature of Advaita can be considered only at arm's length from the aspect of duality, which results in an academic understanding of the subject, much like the idea of freedom as seen from inside the prison cell; a tantalising idea, but an idea that is incapable of delivering the actual experience no matter how deeply it is studied.

For experiencing a taste of Advaita, the instruction could not be simpler: find a quiet place to sit comfortably with a straight back, close your eyes, repeat the Mantra within and follow where it takes you. When meditation is practised with faith and the utter conviction that it leads from darkness to light, it transforms ordinary life by exchanging theory for experience.

> *If you can stand still from Self-thinking and Self-willing, and can stop the wheel of imagination and senses... when both intellect and will are quiet... And if you can for a while cease from thinking and willing, then shall you hear the unspeakable Word of God.* [7]

Meditation leads to direct experience, which is equally beneficial for those on the path of knowledge, the path of love, the path of action, the Fourth Way, and for those who do not subscribe to any path; it is truly universal. The answers found in meditation have no words or concepts, in the same way that joy has no words or concepts; it just nourishes the soul.

> *We were never born and will never die. We have to realise this fact. Feel it, be aware that it is truth. Not a wonderful idea. The truth is, there was never a time when you and I did not exist. What we seek we have always been. I understand a gratitude to people like Dr. Roles and the Shankaracharya who because of their lives create surroundings that are conducive to our own reflections, but at the end of the day we have to see for ourselves that we have invented through thought, the separate existence.* [2]

When asked "What is it that makes me meditate?" the answer was:

It is Buddhi in pure state…Buddhi in pure state reminds one and chases one to work for betterment. Good company enhances the chances of development and bad company would dim it out. [1]

Divesting oneself of all the psychological and emotional baggage that is normally recognised as essential and necessary, is traditionally described as a journey. It can be the journey of a lifetime or, as in meditation, a regular and cumulative familiarisation with the company of Truth.

Meditation by itself is not an isolated act, it is a journey from the start of a mantra to the end of all agitation. This is a bridge over which one needs to throw one's belongings of desires and activities while walking towards the other end… The practice of meditation demands relinquishing activity. At one end of the bridge is the start of an activity and at the other end is the stillness, the immobility. The practice of meditation between these two points is to pick up the mantra, embark on the activity of repetition, and with the help of the mantra, allow everything – even the mantra – to disappear without doing anything extra. The rhythm of activity will settle down to come to a complete stillness – not of a void, but of fullness, which is the presence of the Self. [1]

A bridge, like any one might take, this symbolic bridge differs in that while it carries the road ahead, it also imposes the conditions of the journey. One takes this bridge to overcome obstructions but discovers on the way that one has packed and brought along one's own obstructions.

As the bridge gets higher and narrower, one discovers that in order to progress it is necessary to discard things of which one is very fond. The narrower the bridge becomes the more luggage must be despatched to the chasm. And when the bridge is just a single footpath – no parapet, no rail – one-pointed attention is essential, so stray thoughts have to go as well. Then, fear of falling, fear of losing oneself in the depths, marks the measure of the bonds that remain – the sense of a separate self.

> *Without doubt, if we empty ourselves of all that belongs to the creature, depriving ourselves of it for the love of God, that same Lord will fill us with Himself.* [8]

Whatever is not Self belongs to the world. The world cannot be taken into the silence. What cannot be taken will hold one back if it is not released. In the East, monkeys are trapped by burying a round pot in the ground, leaving only the slender neck protruding. In the pot is a banana which attracts the unfortunate monkey, who then reaches in to take it. Holding on to the fruit, he is unable to withdraw his hand and is held fast by his reluctance to let go. The poor monkey lacks the sense to measure the value of a brief treat against permanent bondage and consequently is a prisoner of his own making.

> *All our desires and volitions come as obstacles in our experiences in meditation, and attention is lost. It would be advisable to ask them [your disciples] to have fewer desires.* [1]

MANTRA

Word is the realisation of meaning expressed in sound. It starts as a concept without form or name or presence. The will to express the concept, propels it into the realm of manifest phenomena where it appears as intelligible sound. That same will is identified by different traditions as the beginning of phenomena. For example, in the Judeo-Christian tradition:

> *In the beginning was the Word, and the Word*
> *was with God, and the Word was God. [9]*

...and in the Hindu tradition of Advaita Vedanta:

> *The Creator begins the act of creation with*
> *meditation. [1]*

Whether the word is translated as *Logos* or *Mantram* really makes no difference at all. If one puts aside the superficial cultural differences and penetrates to the underlying meaning, the reality is that the same single truth is being described.

The progression from unmanifest to manifest, bringing meaning from the subtle world into focus as sound in the phenomenal world, is the same path taken on the return journey back to the source – the journey back home. Within creation, special sounds that manifest the essence of the creative will, signal the path to union. These sounds are the phenomenal representation of primary qualities. Manifest sounds express those qualities at the phenomenal level, unmanifest sounds impart their subtle effects, and the causal properties provide a pathway to their source.

Those who heard this word by the ear alone let it go out by the other ear; but those who heard it with their souls imprinted it on their souls and repeated it until it penetrated their hearts and souls, and their whole beings became this word. They were made independent of the pronunciation of the word; they were released from the sound of the letters. Having understood the spiritual meaning of this word, they became so absorbed in it that they were no more conscious of their own non-existence. [10]

The mantra responds to guileless effort – the meditation comes to meet those who are honest and sincere. By entering the silence in the company of the mantra, one turns from the creation to the Creator and meets Him in the heart as the intimate reflection of one's own True Self. The journey inwards joins the pathway of the Great Meditation, which started before time's first beat and will continue after its last. Like the fountain of knowledge, the Great Meditation has no beginning and no end.

When the mantra makes its home in the heart, its presence is felt as warm companionship – good company – and it is from there, the centre of the physical being, that it makes life beautiful.

Whenever one gets something in the physical world which seems valuable, one likes to keep it in a safe place in such a place that one can easily make use of it, or look at it whenever one feels like it and get some pleasure from it. One sometimes puts them into safes, and whenever the need arises, one takes them out and uses them.

In the same way when we get some big or good idea either from the Grace of the Absolute, or from the Grace of a Realised Man or from the Scriptures, or from Satsang, the best thing to do to preserve it is to keep it in a safe place. The safest place is the heart itself... Only the wise can keep it in their heart because the fool assembles all the rubbish which he collects and keeps that in his heart. [1]

Life itself is a meditation on whatever is stored in the heart. Every sound contains the potential to manifest its meaning. Expression of sound, particularly repetition of unmanifest sound at the subtle level, crystallises its meaning. All life is driven from the heart's desire, and repetition upon repetition of what is in one's heart is meditation on the timescale of a life. What lives in the heart is what one meditates on and what one meditates on is what one acquires. Kept in the heart are the things held closest and dearest; the things that direct one's attitude to daily activities and upon which the shape of a life is formed.

How do we know what is kept in the heart? Anything which we remember again and again and seek for... This is how one can check if the thing has been placed in the heart or not. [1]

The sage Vyasa, who compiled the Bhagavad-Gita said: "I have made a critical study of all the Scriptures several times. The gist of all that, as I found, is that we should hold the Universal Self in memory all the time."

A wife will recognise the voice of her husband in a multitude; a disciple will recognise the voice of his teacher in a multitude. Vyasa recognised the voice of Krishna on the battlefield. In the same way, one who is really searching for the True Self will hear and recognise the Voice of Truth amid the multitude of desires, ambitions and duties created by the mind.

> *You have been provided with the meditation and the mantra, and in this is the same power and vision as the teacher's. You have also been provided with True Knowledge and a system of discipline. Not only the words, but the power of the words to nourish you has also been provided. It is up to everybody to remove the obstacles and impediments for themselves......the rest is up to you...* [1]

> *..."Indeed", continued the Hoopoe, "I can think of no better fortune for a valiant man than that he loses himself from himself."* [11]

SOME QUESTIONS & ANSWERS

Q Why am I interested in meditation – where does that interest come from?

A People experience a lack of wholeness which leads to questions about the purpose and meaning of things they see around them and what they feel within – things and feelings which seem unjust, empty or incomplete. The impression of incompleteness comes about because of an instinctive sense that it should be normal to feel whole, relaxed and joyful. That instinct comes from the connection everyone has to the true nature of existence. People are unaware of that connection because it is overwhelmed by individual personality. Nevertheless, rising through one's personality, that connection prompts one to realise one's true nature and that prompting is the cause of your interest.

Q Why seek to know one's true nature? Surely I already know who I am?

A We call ourselves 'I' but the I who asks this question will at some point become the I who is interested in something else. The I who is confident will become the I who feels awkward. The I who loves will become the I who hates. These experiences of 'I' are transient, they change all the time so they cannot be real. If they are not real then what are they? They are illusions superimposed on the truth. The truth is who you really are.

Q So how does one find truth?

A No one finds the truth because everyone already is the

truth. People are like actors who remain in character all the time, cannot leave the stage or get out of costume. They have forgotten their real identity so they just go on repeating the lines they have learnt – the lines of a fool or the lines of a sage, it makes no difference. It is not a question of finding anything but of realising one's true Self.

Q   How do we discover our true identity?

A   Before you can be who you are, you must come out of who you are not. Who you are and who you are not is explained like this:

> There is only one consciousness; everything is that consciousness; the levels are levels of impediment to that consciousness. [12]

Those levels of impediment are the theatre of activity for ordinary life. They are the levels where theory and philosophy belong, and where people disagree and quarrel. It stands to reason, that as long as the search for '*one consciousness*' seeks it in the '*levels of impediment to that consciousness*' the search will encounter only impediments – sophistry, conjecture, delusion, superstition etc. Meditation is a technique for stepping out of these impediments.

Q   Sometimes I find I am too busy to meditate.

A   You are never too busy, too late or too tired to meditate. Meditation makes life more efficient and brings energy and relief. One only gains, never loses.

Q I feel I am not making progress.

A You must understand that no effort is wasted. Understand that and you will persevere. Faith in the meditation is fundamental to answering many of the questions that arise when people look for meaning in life. The meditation doesn't provide explanations, but by shining a light on problems that live only in the dark, it shows that much that troubles us doesn't really exist.

Q Why a straight back?

A Posture when meditating is most important. Unless the back is straight the mantra won't travel around freely. The more subtle the mantra becomes, the more it spreads through the body. As you go on pronouncing the mantra, it moves deeper – going slower and slower, spreading through the whole of the body until it merges completely into the Self, into the source from which it came. Whether sitting on a chair or on the ground, the posture – Asana – should be erect. As an entertainer balances an object on the tip of a finger by keeping it upright, so should the back be upright. One should not interfere with the natural curves of the spine; just feel it relaxed, supported and erect. Poor posture leads to sleep. If the Mantra doesn't travel people lose faith and stop meditating.

Q What does it mean: life is a meditation on what is in the heart?

A When one reflects on the same things with the same attitudes, day after day, year after year, it leaves an impression – a heart's desire – that influences life to the extent that it shapes what one becomes. Meditation fills the heart with joy which manifests in the wider world as love, compassion, understanding etc. and is evident in the lives and actions of those who are free.

Q   We are told: love thy neighbour. What if you don't feel love?

A   Many people express this concern. Do not worry on that account. Love and truth are different names for the same thing which is the nature of the Self – your Self and the Self of the universe. When we speak of feeling love, we speak of a person experiencing a feeling and the two are separate. The injunction to 'love thy neighbour as thyself' refers to the universal truth that in reality there is no separation. The Brihadaranyaka Upanishad says: *Your own True Self dwells in the hearts of all; nothing else matters.* Once this is absorbed as true, there is no further question about love; love is what you are.

Q   What can you say about the initiation ceremony?

A   Only the initiate and the initiator are present when the mantra is given.

*   *   *

Thanks to
The Society for the Study of Normal Psychology
www.studysociety.com
for permission to quote from
A Record of Audiences with
His Holiness Swami Shantananda Saraswati
Shankaracharya of Jyotirmath

Cover illustration of
Nebula NGC 2174 in the constellation of Orion
courtesy of
NASA/Hubble Space Telescope

NOTES

Notes in the text refer to extracts from the following:

1   A record of audiences with His Holiness Swami
     Shantananda Saraswati, Shankaracharya of Jyotirmath

2   Private correspondence with the author

3   Traditional: translated from the Vedanta by
     Swami Shivananda

4   The White Book: T Brass

5   The Sufi Message: Hazrat Inayat Khan quoting
     Saadi Shirazi

6   The Mathnawi, Book 3: 28: JalaludDin Rumi

7   The Supersensual Life: Jacob Boehme

8   The Interior Castle, Seventh Mansion Ch2: 9: Saint
     Teresa of Ávila,

9   The New Testament of The Bible: John 1:1

10 From the sayings of Abu Sa'id

11 The Conference of the Birds: Farid ud-Din Attar

12 Dr. Francis Roles